Teach My Preschooler
How To Read Book 3
DIAGRAPHS - Two - Three - Four
Letter Consonant Sounds

Author: Paul Mackie

Written and illustrated by Paul Mackie.

Library and Archives Canada Cataloguing in Publication

Mackie, Paul - Author
TEACH MY PRESCHOOLER HOW TO READ BOOK 3

ISBN: 978-1-988986-30-2 (softcover)

Copyright© 2021 by Paul Mackie

Educationalchildsplay@gmail.com

NOTE: In educational settings, coloring pages can be copied for children to color.

Contents

Contents

HOW TO TEACH PRESCHOOL CHILDREN TO READ
THE PRESCHOOL READING PROCESS

- Preschool children learn through play.
- Give your child a letter sound picture to color.
- Point to and say the large upper page letter sound.
- Point to each picture and say the picture name, while extending the first letter sound of the picture; as in ("ch"   "o-p") or ("ch"   "i-p-s").
- Point to the large upper page letter sound and ask your child, "What letter sound is this?"
- Sound out the page letter sound, then sound out each lowercase letter sound in the word (example: "ch" then "o" and "p"); ask your child to fill in the underlined letters to the word.
- Trace the letter sound with your finger and ask your child to trace and say the letter sound.

In "TEACH MY PRESCHOOLER HOW TO READ BOOK 1 – PHONICS abc coloring book your child learned the 26 letter sounds of the English Alphabet and should be able to phonetically sound out and write the lower-case letter sounds.

In "TEACH MY PRESCHOOLER HOW TO READ BOOK 2 – Vowels and Sight Words coloring book, your child learns the 5 short and long sound of vowels and the pre-Primer Sight Words: a, and, away, big, blue, can, come, down, find, for, funny, go, help, here, I, in, is, it, jump, little, look, make, me, my, not, one, play, red, run, said, see, the, three, to, two, up, we, where, yellow, you.

In "TEACH MY PRESCHOOLER HOW TO READ BOOK 3 coloring book you are teaching two-three or four letter blended consonant diagraph sounds.
Your child will learn 38 of the most common blended consonant sounds: ch, sh, th, wh, ai, ay, ea, ee, ie, oe, oa, ue, igh, ow, ou, er, ang, kn, wr, mb, dge, oo, oy, oi, or, ar, ear, ir, ur, aw, au, ck, ph, ti, ey, ew, ough, ui.

The 21 consonant Alphabet sounds, 5 vowels and 38 Blended Consonant sounds make up a large percentage of the English language.

REMEMBER: You are teaching children the letter sounds and not the words shown on the pages.

 NOTE: The words printed at the bottom of each page are there to assist you in recognizing what the picture is; you are not teaching these words to your child.

 Over time your child will be able to fill in the words with the letter sounds as sight words or words that can be phonetically sounded out.

HOW TO TEACH PRESCHOOL CHILDREN TO READ
THE PRESCHOOL READING PROCESS

Preschool children learn through play.

Give your child coloring pencils and a picture page to color.

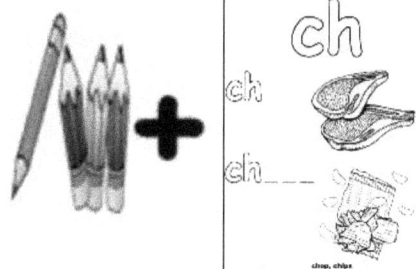

Point to and say the large upper page letter sound ("ch").

Point to each picture and say the picture sound, as in ("ch" "op") or ("ch" "ips"). Sound out the first two letters first then the rest of the word.

Point to the large upper page letter sound and ask your child, "What letter sound is this?"

Once your child knows the letter sound, sound out the letter sound "ch" then sound out each letter sound in the word "o" and "p"; ask your child to fill in the letters to the word.

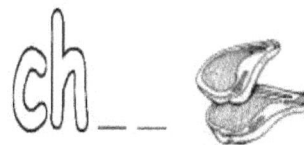

Trace the letter sound with your finger and ask your child to trace and say the letter sound; (first step in learning to write).

ch

ch _ _

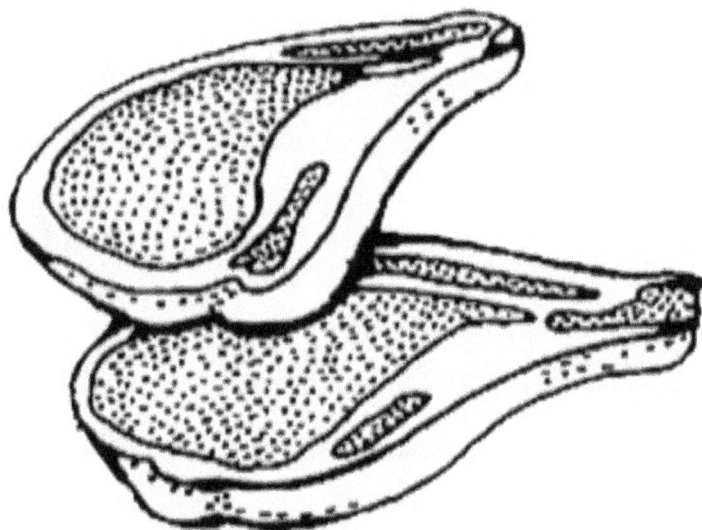

ch _ _ _

chop, chips

sh

___ sh

sh ___

fish, ship

th

__ th
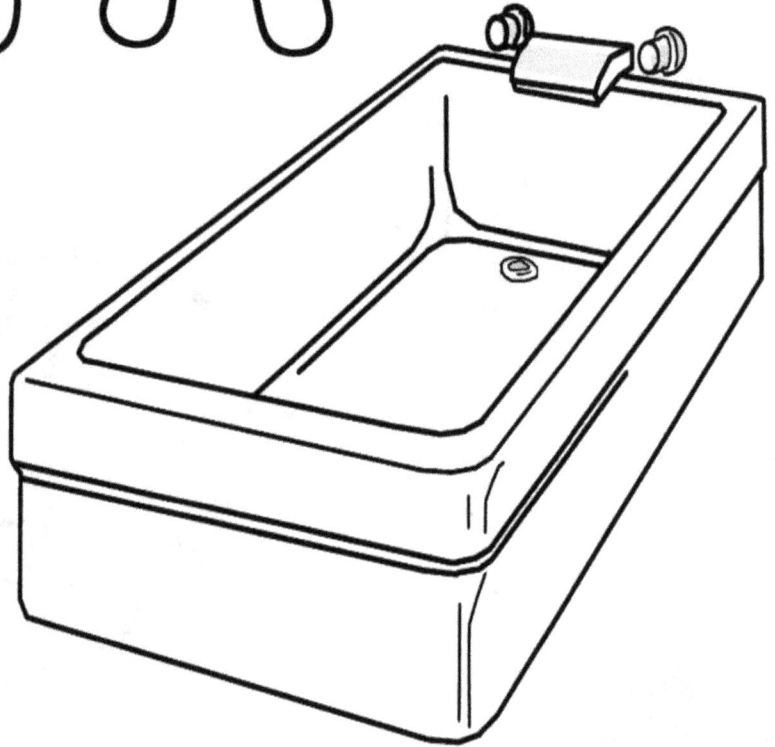

__ th

bath, moth

wh

wh _ _ _ _

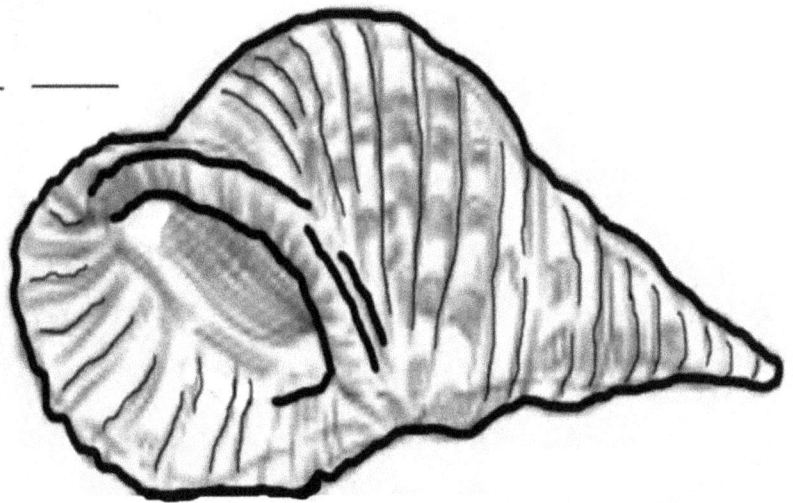

wh _ _ _ _

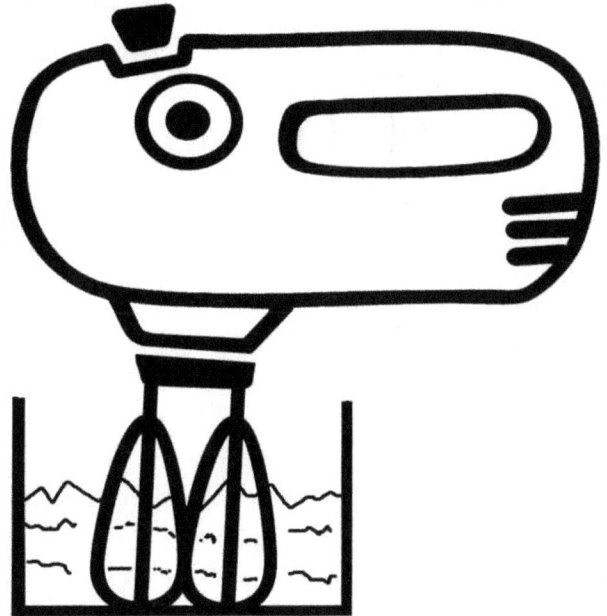

whelk, whisk

ai

ai

ai

train, nail

ay

__ __ ay

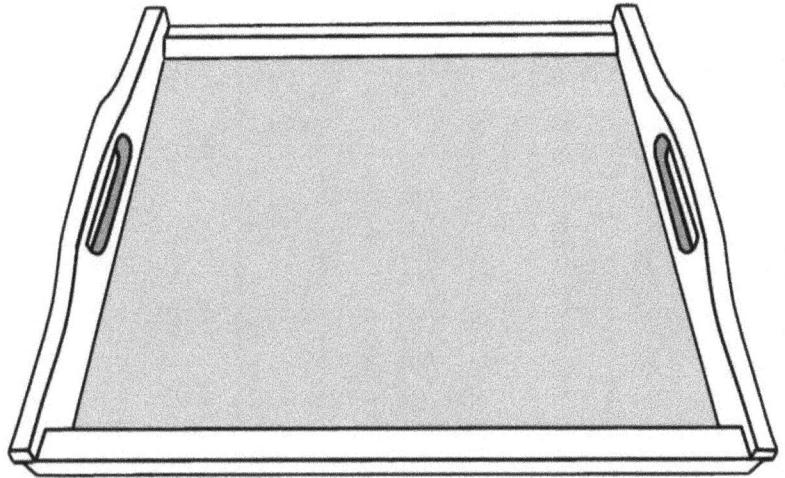

__ __ ay

tray, play

ea

ea_

_ea_

ear, read

ee

__ __ee__

__ee__

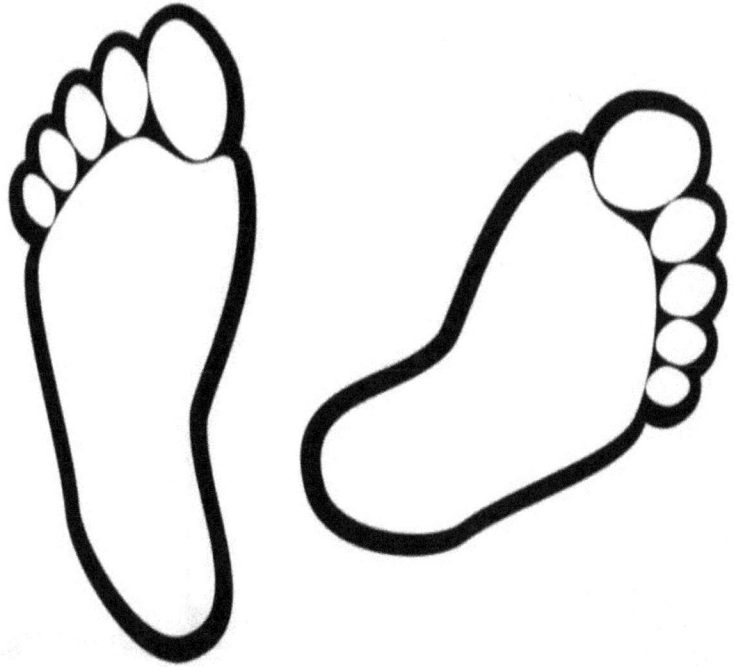

sleep, feet

ie

_ie

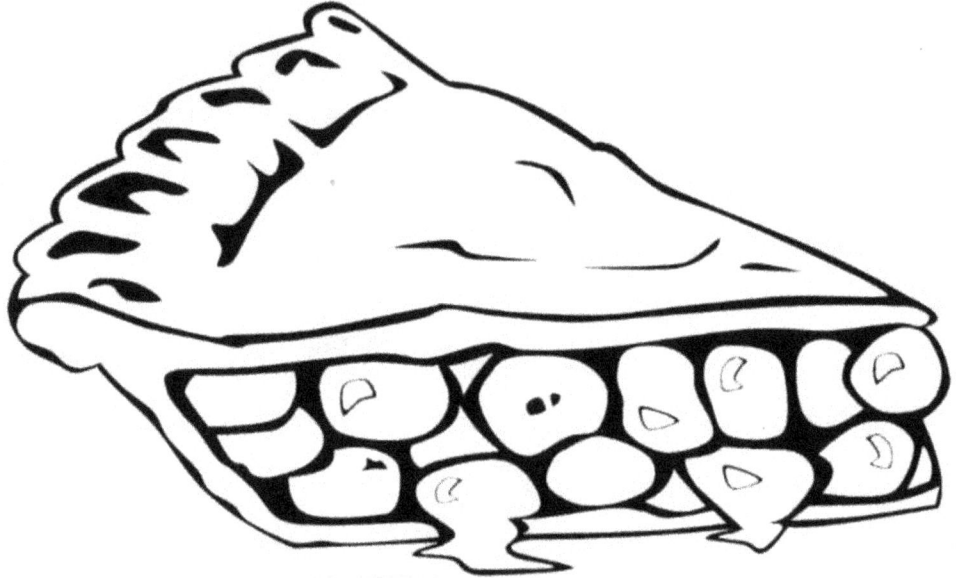

_ie

pie, tie

oe

_oe

_oe

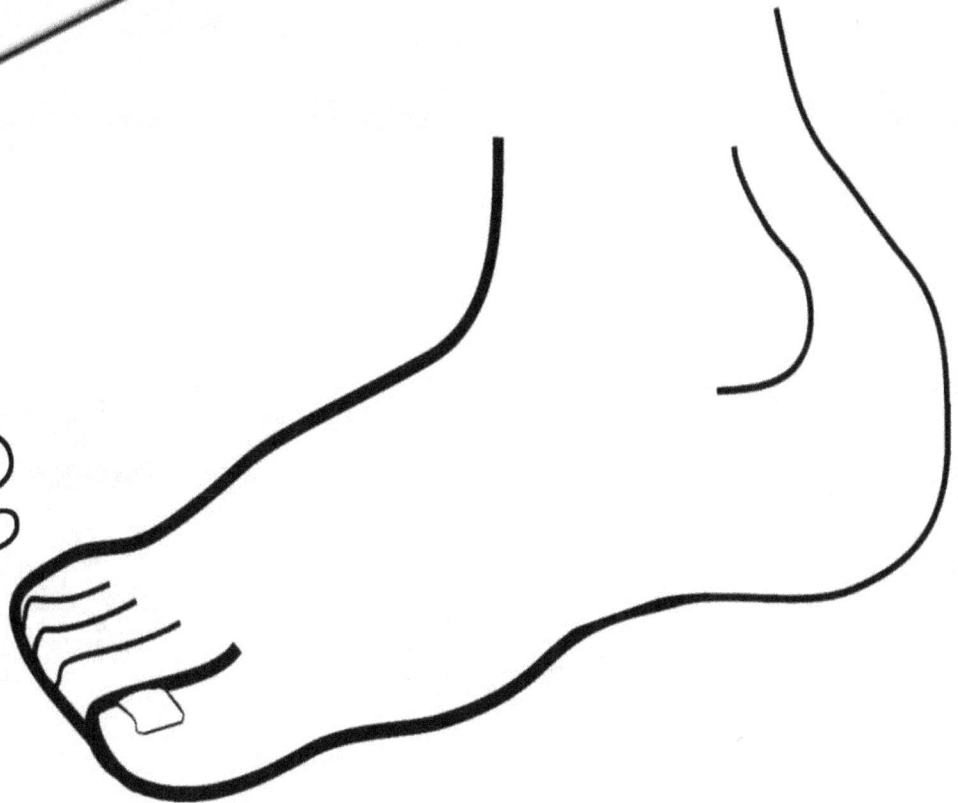

hoe, toe

oa

_oa_

_oa_

coat, boat

ue

___ue

__ue

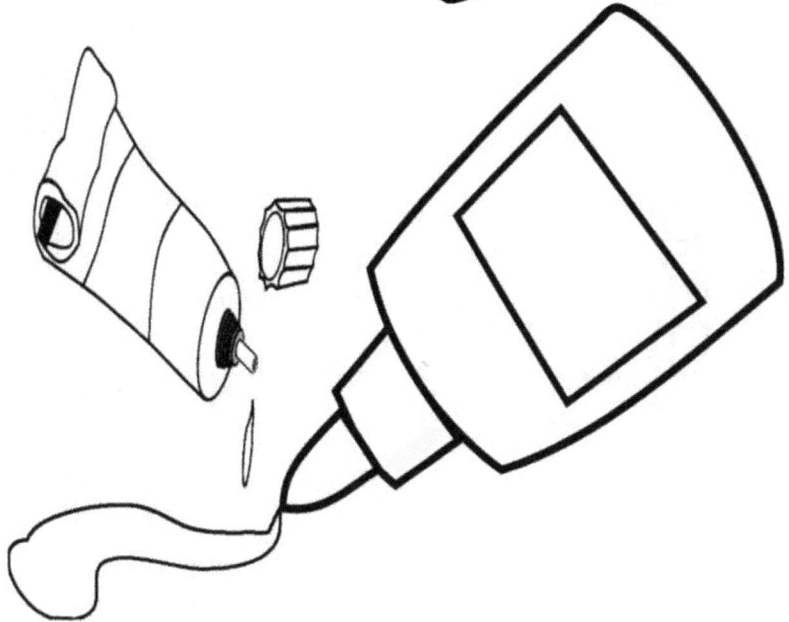

statue, glue

igh

igh

igh

light, fight

OW

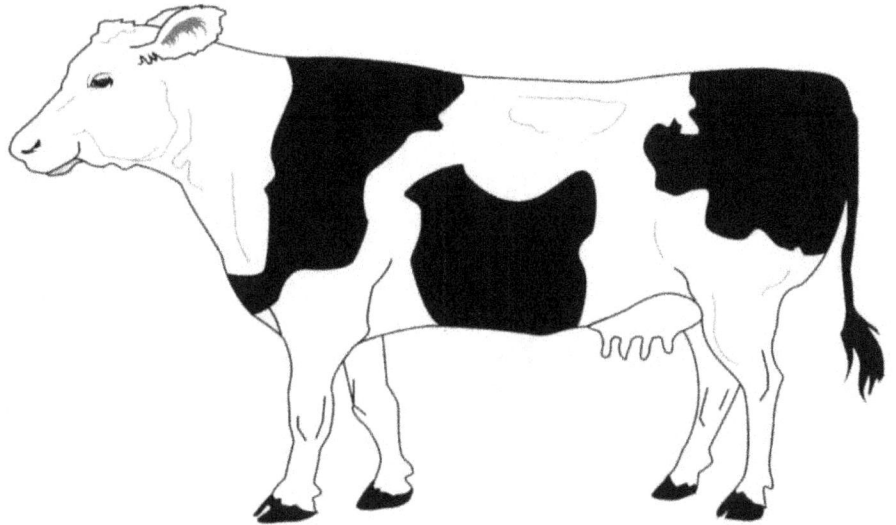

_OW

__ __OW_

cow, clown

ou

ou

_ _ _ ou _

_ _ _ ou _

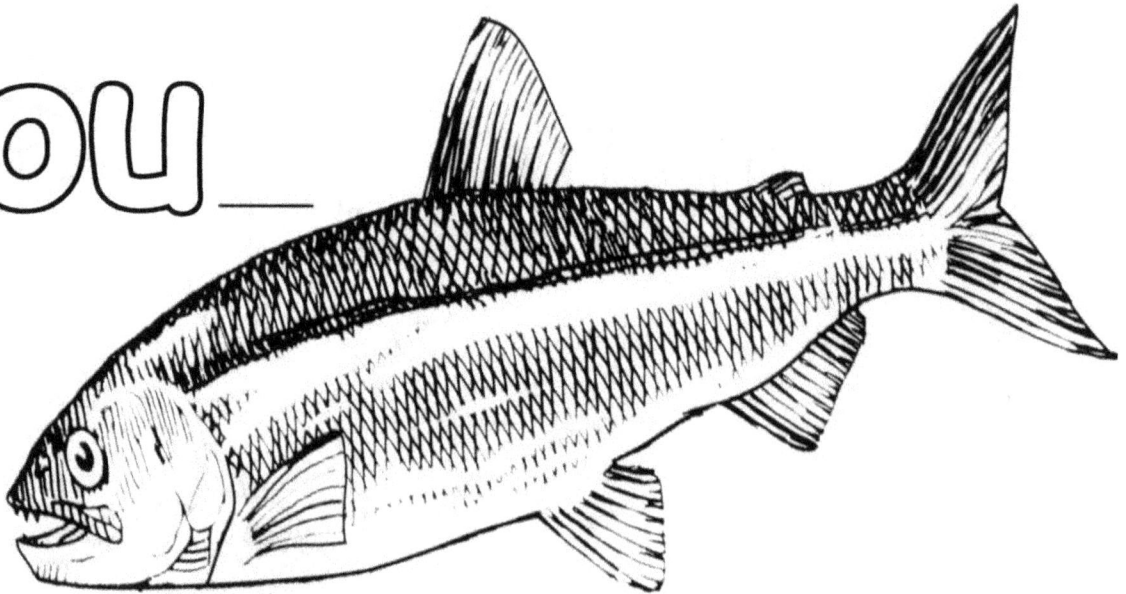

cloud, trout

er

er

_____ er

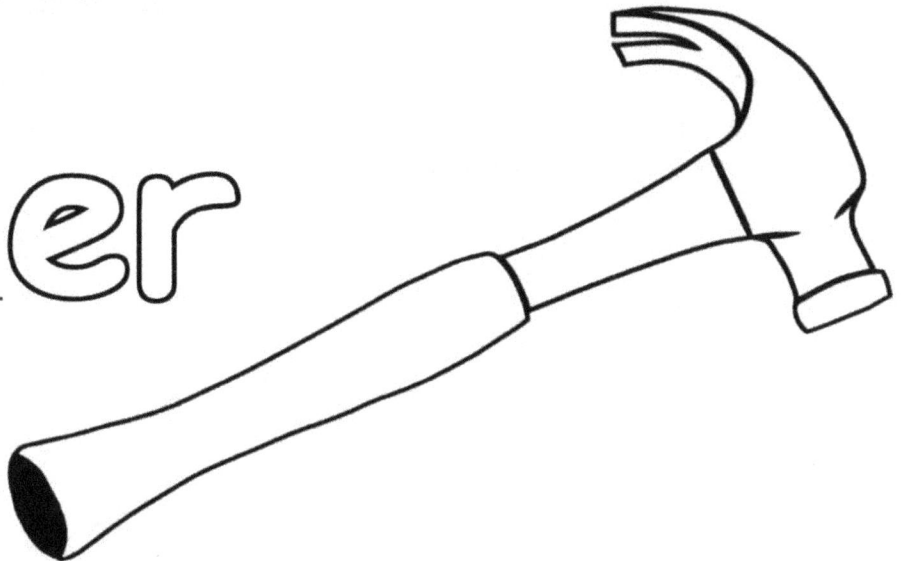

dinner, hammer

ang

ang

ang

mango, fangs

kn

kn _____

kn _____

knitting, knot

wr

wr_ _ _ _

wr_ _ _

wrist, wrap

mb

___ mb

___ mb

lamb, comb

dge

____ dge

____ dge

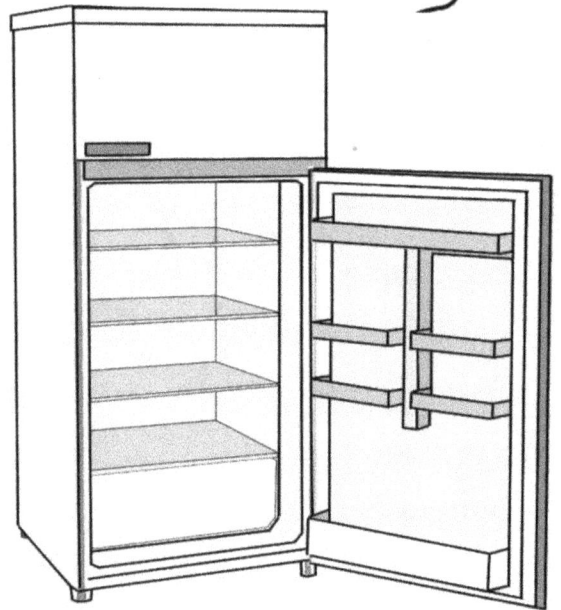

bridge, fridge

OO

___ OO ___

___ OO ___

spoon, broom

OY

_OY

_OY

toy, boy

Oi

_oi_

_oi_____

coin, toilet

or

_or_

_____or_

fork, doctor

ar

_ar

_ar_

jar, farm

ear

_ear

__ear

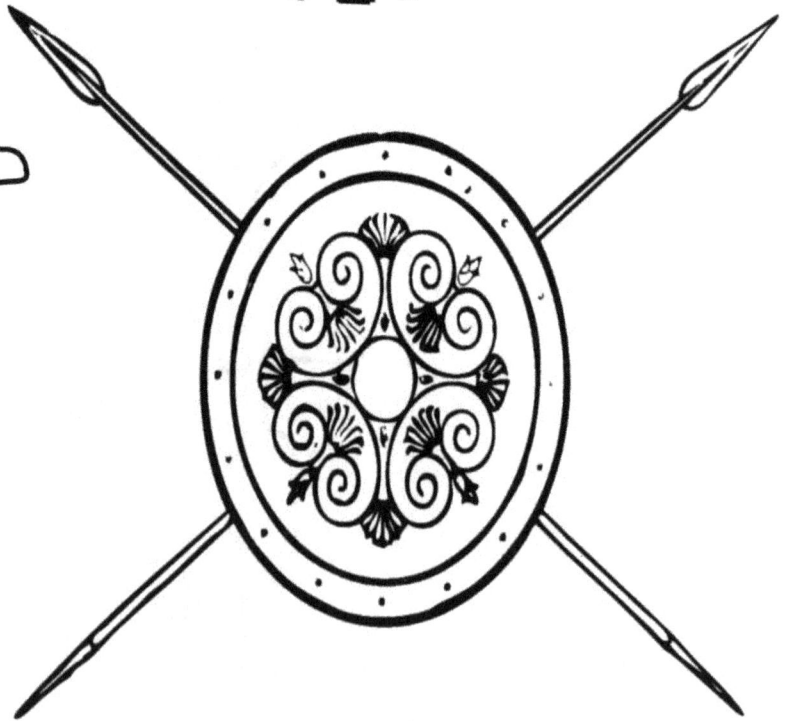

gear, spear

ur

ur

_ur_

ur_

burn, urn

ir

_ir_

_ir_

bird, girl

aw

_ _ _ aw

_ _ aw_

draw, crawl

au

_au_____ _____

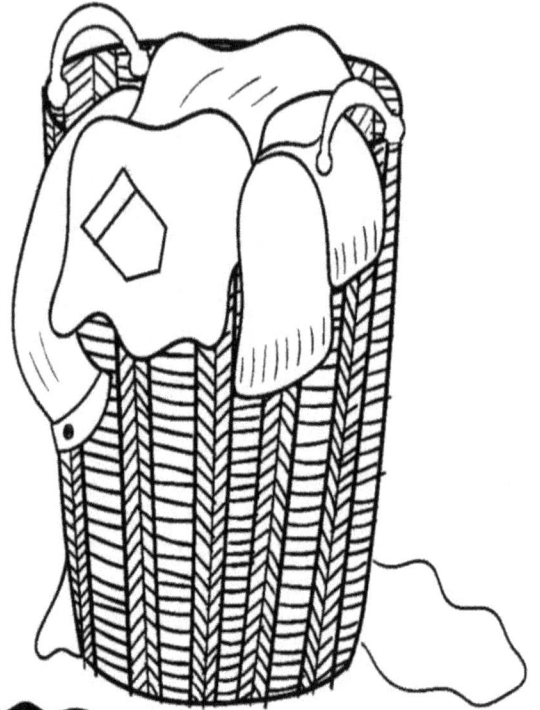

_au_____ _____

laundry, faucet

ck

_ _ ck

_ _ _ ck

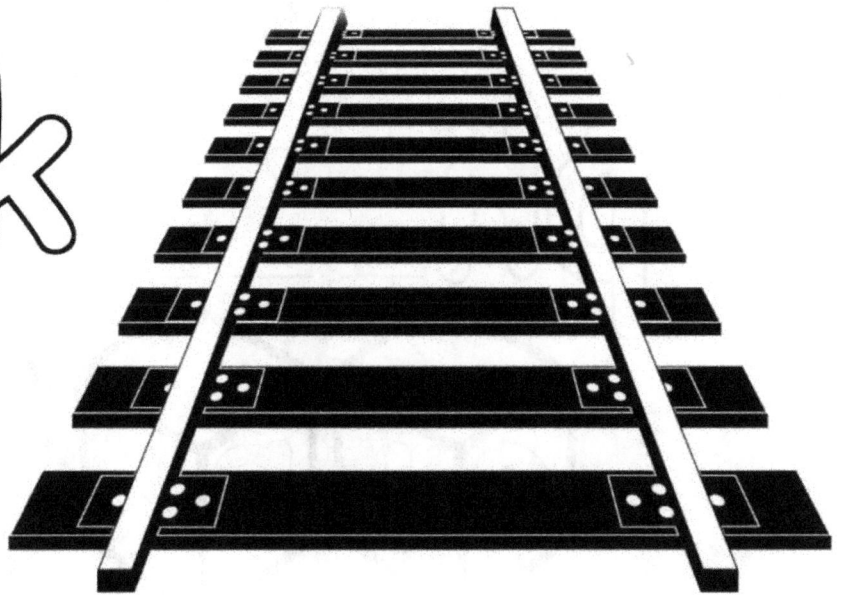

lock, track

ph

ph

ph

elephant, alphabet

ti

ti_

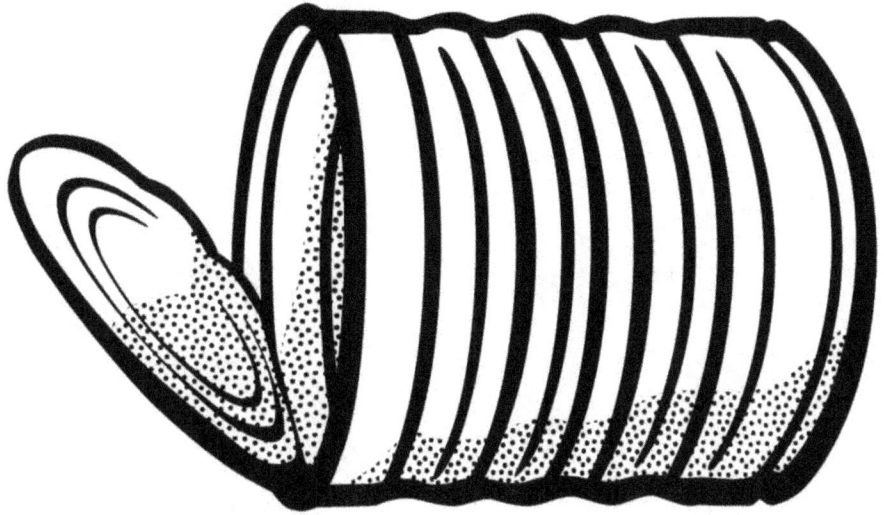

___ ___ ti_ ___ ___

tin, rafting

ey

_ _ _ _ _ _ ey

_ey

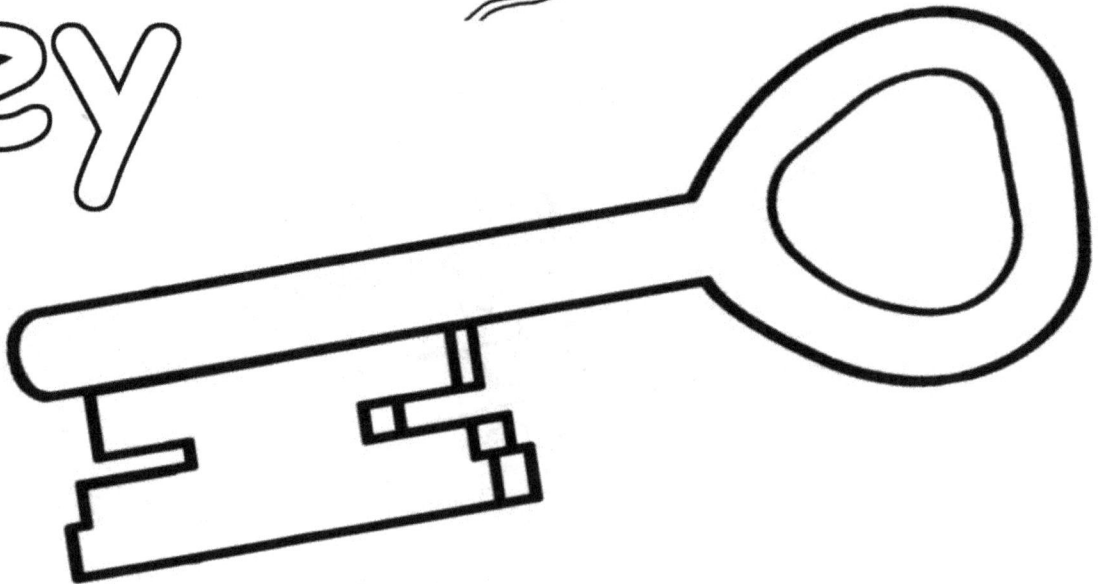

donkey, key

ew

___ ew

__ ew

screw, stew

ough

ough

_ough

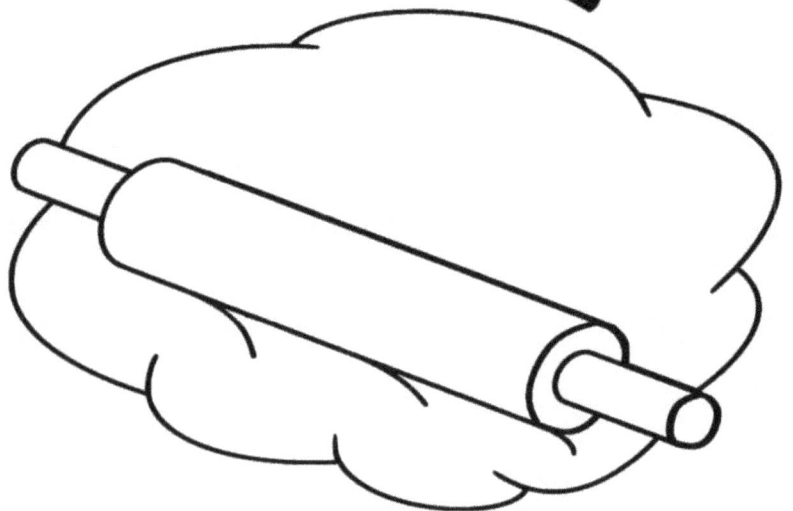

doughnut, dough

ui

_ ui _

_ _ ui _

suit, fruit

ch sh th wh ai ay ea ee

ie oe oa ue igh ow ou er

ang kn wr mb dge oo oy

oi or ar ear ur ir aw au

ck ph ti ey ew ough ui

ch

ch ___ ___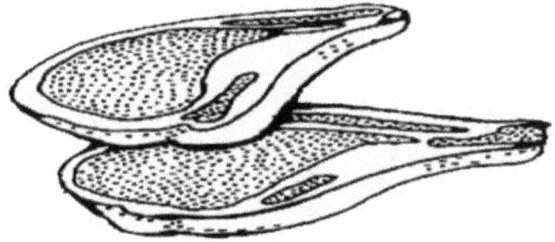

ch ___ ___ ___

ch ___ ___ ___

___ ___ ___ ch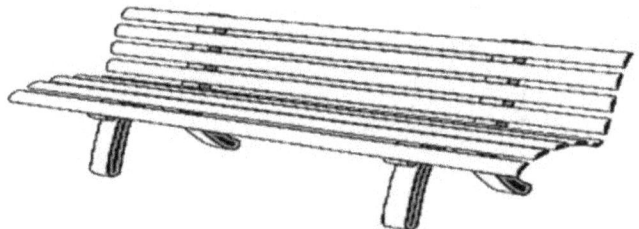

chop, chair, chips, bench

sh

sh _ _

_ _ sh

sh _ _ _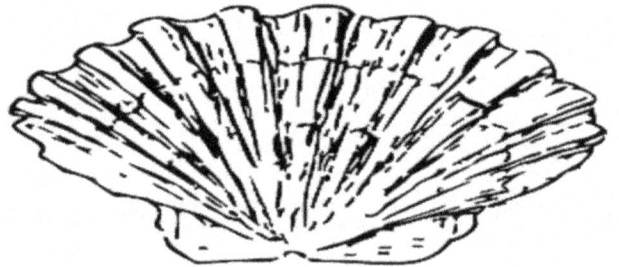

sh _ _

shoe, fish, shell, ship

th

__ __ th

th __ __ __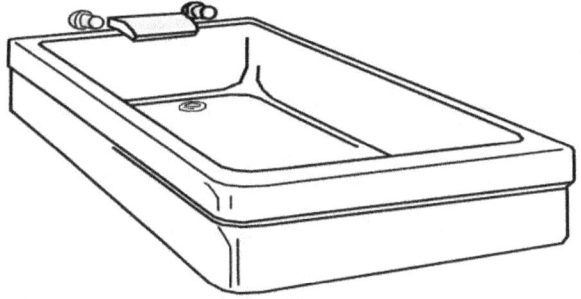

th __ __ __

th __ __

__ __ th

bath, thick, thin, moth

wh

wh _ _ _ _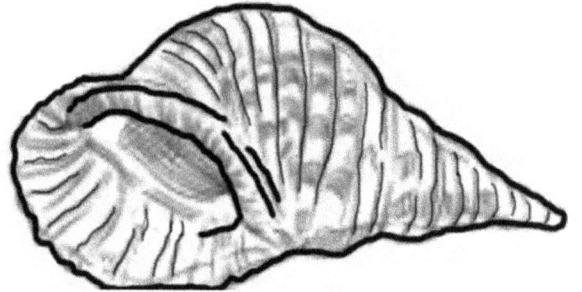

wh _ _ _ _

wh _ _ _ _

wh _ _ _ _ _ _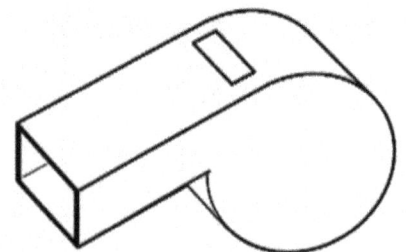

whelk, wheat, whisk, whistle

ai

ai

ai

ai

ai

train, nail, rain, chain

ay

__ ay

__ ay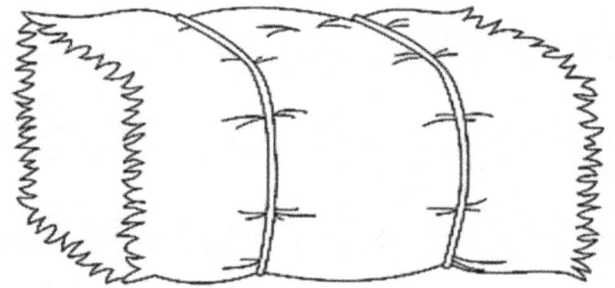

___ __ ay

___ __ ay

lay, hay, tray, play

ea

ea_

ea_

_ea

_ea_

ear, eat, tea, read

ee

_ _ _ee_

_ _ _ee_

_ee_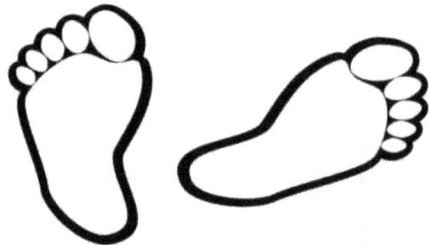

_ _ _ee

sleep, sheep, feet, tree

ie

_ie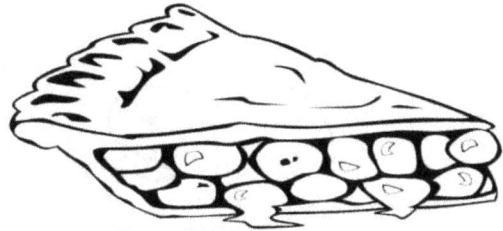

_ie

___ie

_ie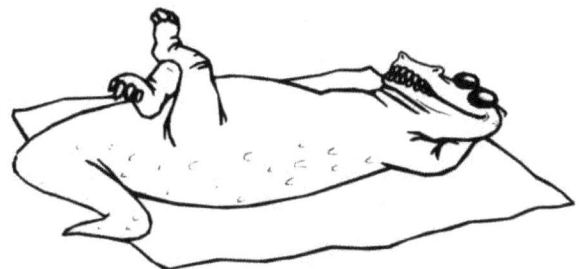

pie, tie, magpie, lie

oe

__ __ __ oe

__ oe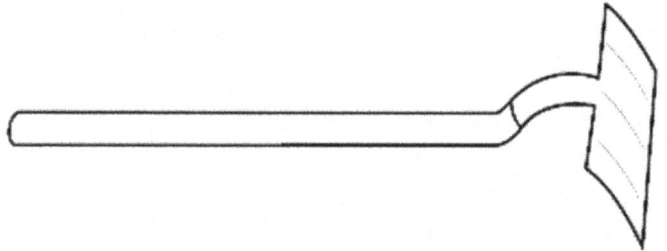

__ __ __ __ __ __ oe

__ oe

shoe, hoe, canoe, toe

oa

_oa_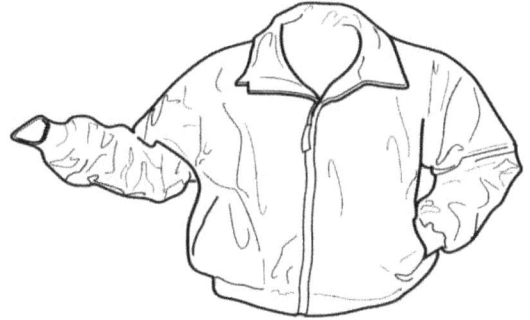

_oa_

_oa_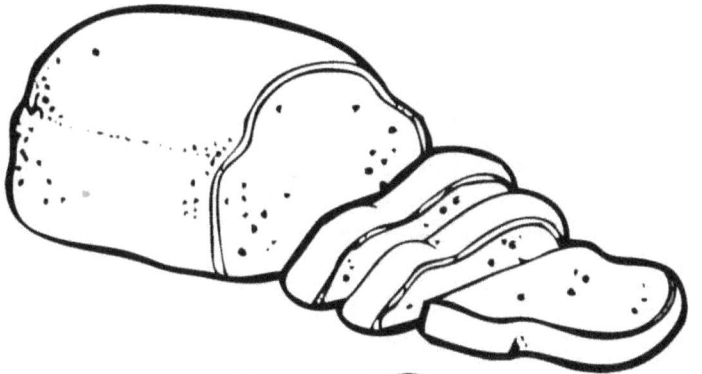

_oa_

coat, boat, loaf, goat

ue

_ _ _ _ _ ue

_ ue _

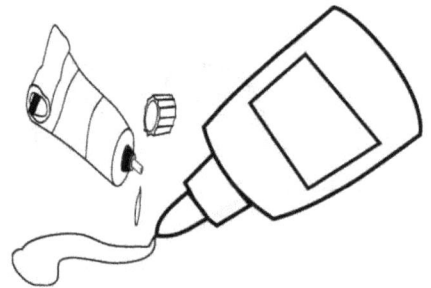

_ _ ue

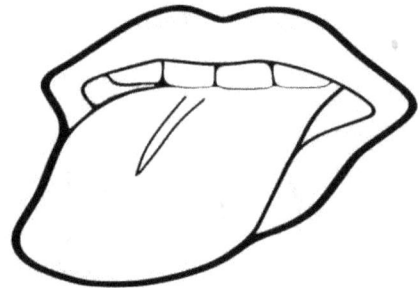

_ _ _ _ _ ue

statue, fuel, glue, tongue

igh

_ _ _ igh _

_ igh _

_ igh _

_ igh _

weight, light, eight, fight

OW

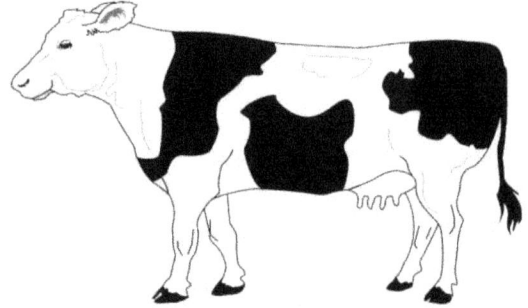

_ OW

_ _ OW _

_ _ OW _

OW _

cow, clown, crown, owl

ou

___ ___ ou ___

___ ou ___ ___

___ ou ___ ___

___ ___ ou ___

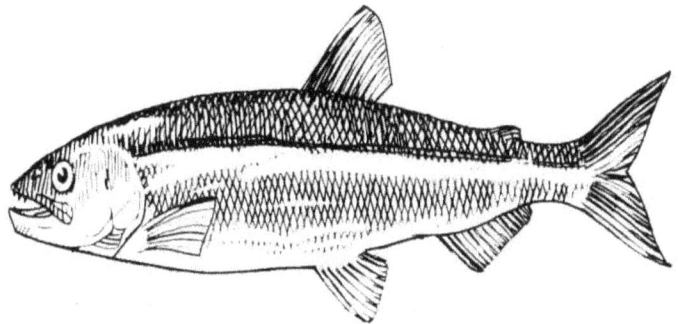

cloud, house, mouse, trout

er

_ _ _ _ _ er

_ _ _ _ _ er

_ _ _ _ _ er

_ _ _ _ _ er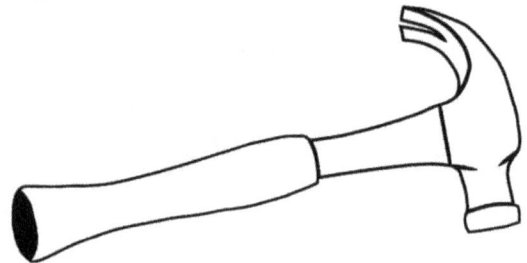

dinner, easter, flower, hammer

ang

ang

ang

ang

ang

mango, kangaroo, fangs, hanger

kn

kn _ _ _ _ _ _

kn _ _ _ _

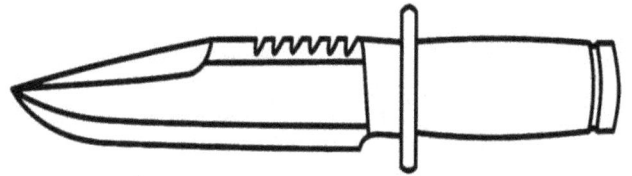

kn _ _ _ _ _ _ _ _

kn _ _ _

knight, knife, knitting, knot

wr

wr _ _ _

wr _ _ _ _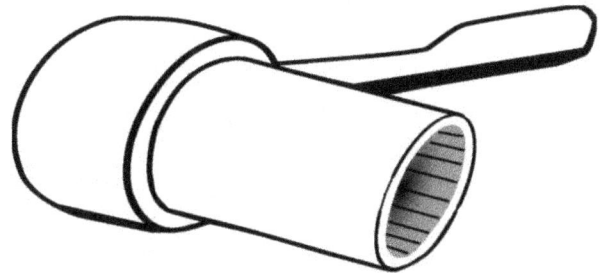

wr _ _

wr _ _ _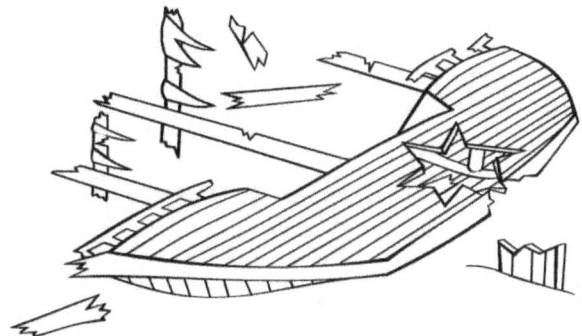

wrist, wrench, wrap, wreck

mb

___ mb

___ mb ___

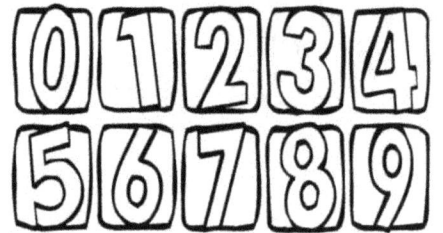

___ mb ___

___ mb

lamb, numbers, plumber, comb

dge

dge

_____

dge

_____

dge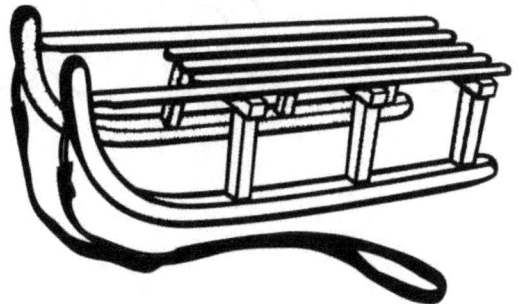

_____

dge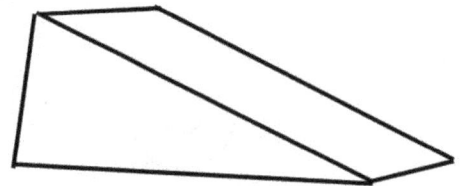

bridge, fridge, sledge, wedge

OO

_ OO _ _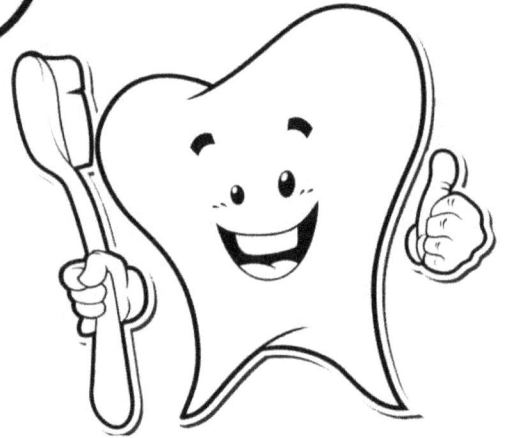

_ OO _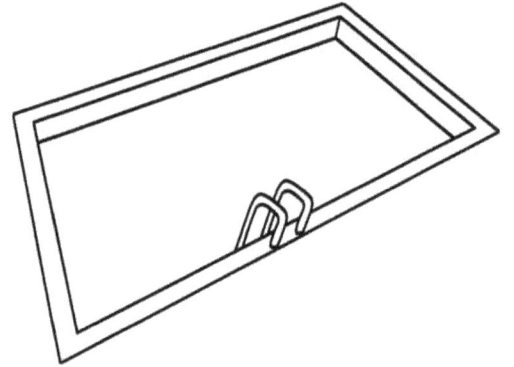

_ _ OO _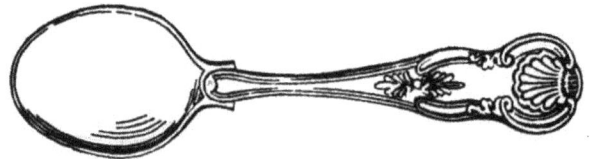

_ _ OO _

tooth, pool, spoon, broom

OY

_OY

_OY

_____OY

OY_____

toy, boy, cowboy, oyster

oi

_oi_

_oi_ _ _

oi_ _ _ _

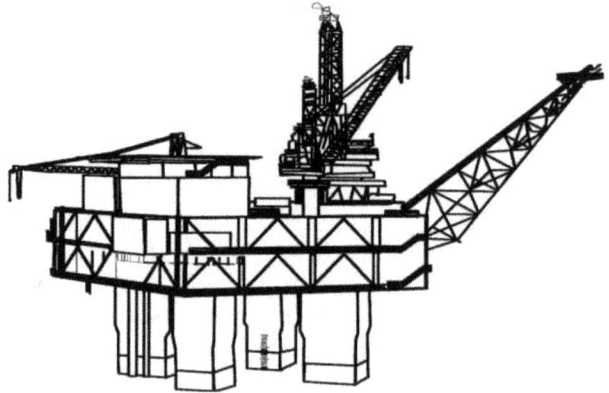

_ _ _ _ oi_ _

coin, toilet, oil rig, tortoise

or

_or_ _

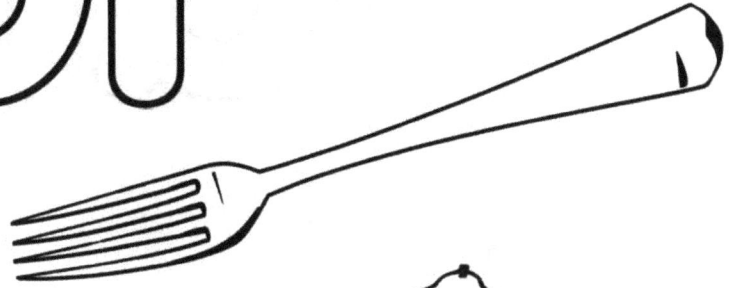

__or_ _

_____or _

_or_ _

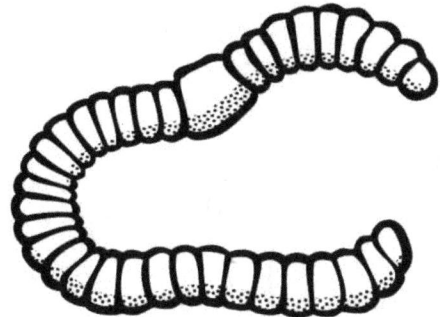

fork, acorn, doctor, worm

ar

_ar

_____ _ar

_ar_____

_ar_

jar, calendar, garbage, farm

ear

_ ear

_ _ ear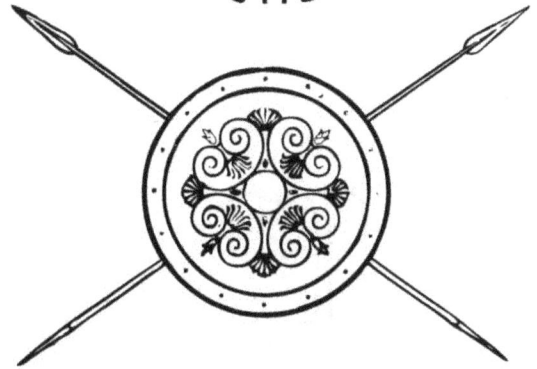

ear_ _ _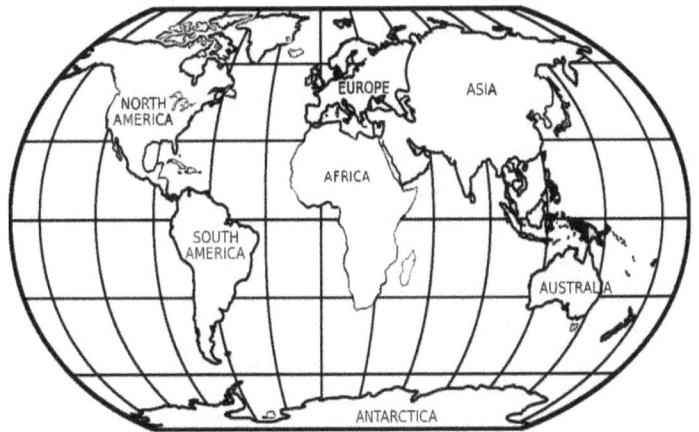

_ ear

gear, spear, earth, bear

ur

_ur_

_ur___

_ur____

ur_

burn, nurse, turtle, urn

ir

_ir__

_ir__

__ir_

__ir_

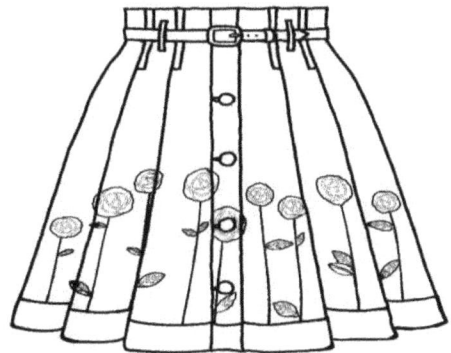

bird, girl, shirt, skirt

aw

_ _ _ aw

_ aw

_ _ _ aw _

_ aw _

draw, saw, crawl, hawk

74

au

_au_ _ _ _

_au_ _ _ _ _ _

_au_ _ _ _ _

_au_ _ _ _ _ _

sauce, laundry, saucer, faucet

ck

_ _ ck

_ _ ck_ _

_ _ ck

_ _ _ _ ck

lock, jockey, dock, track

ph

ph _ _ _ _

_ _ _ _ ph _ _ _ _

ph _ _ _ _ _ _

_ _ _ ph _ _ _ _

phone, elephant, pheasant, alphabet

ti

ti__ __

__ __ __ ti__ __

__ __ __ __ ti__ __

ti__

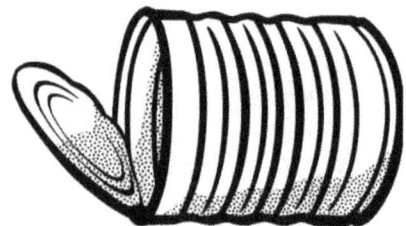

time, artist, rafting, tin

ey

_ _ _ _ _ _ ey

_ ey

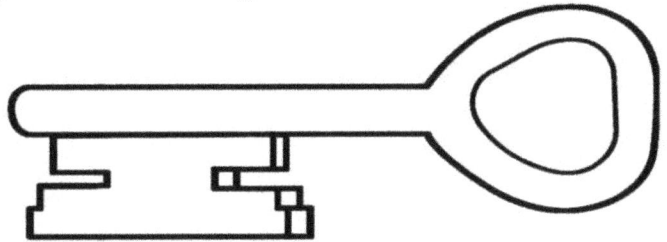

ey _

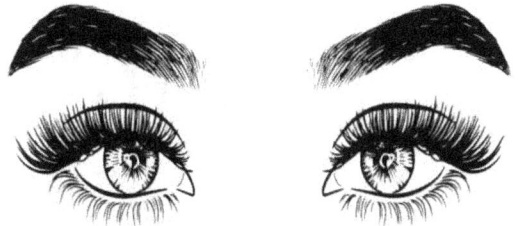

_ _ ey _ _ _ _

donkey, key, eye, greyhound

ew

_ _ _ _ ew

_ ew _

_ _ ew

_ _ _ ew

screw, news, stew, chew

ough

_ough___ _

___ough

_ough

_ough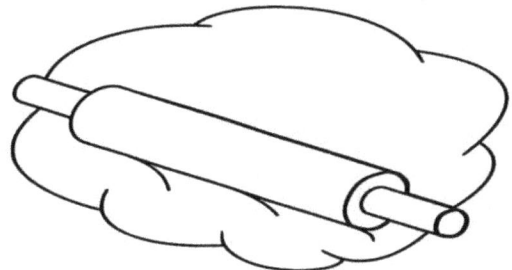

doughnut, plough, cough, dough

ui

_ _ ui _

_ _ ui _

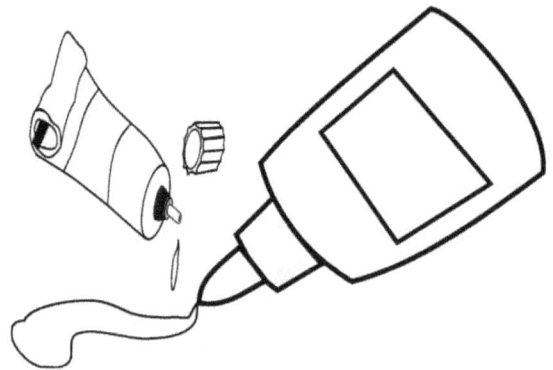

_ _ ui _ _

suit, squid, gluing, fruit

OTHER BOOKS BY THE AUTHOR

https://www.amazon.com/author/paulmackie
https://howtoteachchildrentoread.ca/

	A WALK IN THE JUNGLE - Storybook Prepare preschool children emotionally, intellectually and physically, before they go to grade school. Give your child an unprecedented, LIFELONG advantage, simply by reading them a storybook; a storybook UNLIKE ANY OTHER you've seen before. It feels so good to see your child achieve milestones, absorb knowledge like a sponge and develop a true love of learning.
	GORDY VISITS THE MOUTAINS - Storybook Gordy Visits The Mountains helps children develop physical coordination; improves self-direction; enhances decision making; and promotes problem solving. A fun play-based child development storybook activity gets your child ready to learn.
	LEO LEARNS TO READ - Storybook Leo Learns To Read shows you how to teach the fundamentals of reading. This storybook helps children learn the fundamental keys to reading, and gives children the exciting gift, that they are "Reading to Learn".
	ALPHABET PARK -Storybook This story is designed to teach children the basics of reading; so, they will learn to read, and then "read to learn". Each page has a story about a letter of the alphabet; then there is either a question about the story, or a movement activity; children are asked to write the sound of the alphabet letter.

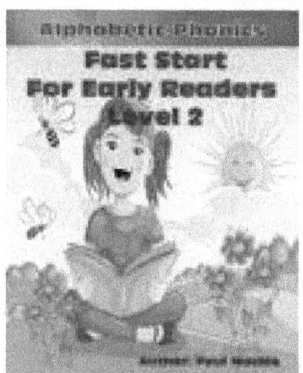

	FAST START FOR EARLY READERS KINDERGARTEN This book introduces preschool children to the Alphabet letter sounds in picture form; children quickly and easily learn to read most three letter words. This book shows you how to develop your child's "ear", "tongue", "eye" and "word building" skills, so that your child will quickly be able to read most three letter words.
	FAST START FOR EARLY READERS LEVEL 1 This book introduces short sentences using the phonetic sounds of the alphabet and pre primer sight words. The book has large easy to read letters and matching black and white pictures to help preschool children easily learn to read.
	FAST START FOR EARLY READERS LEVEL 2 With this book children learn how to read four or more word punctuated sentences; recognize 26 letter sounds of the alphabet; as well as 92 Pre-Primer Sight Words.
	PLAY-BASED WAYS TO TEACH YOUR CHILD TO READ This book shows you: What play based toys and learning to read materials to use. A step by step plan to teach your child to read and write showing you; how to present learning to read materials to your child: how to present learning to write materials to your child; that learning to read and write can be fun and play-based; how to set up the in-home reading and writing environment; that pre-school children can learn to read and write.

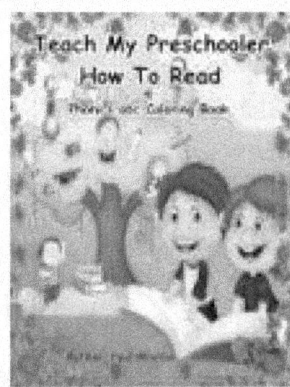

	TEACH MY PRESCHOOLER HOW TO READ PHONICS abc COLORING BOOK Preschool children learn: The 26 letter sounds of the English Alphabet; how to phonetically sound out 3 letter words; how to read most phonetic sounding 3 letter words; how to write 26 English Alphabet letters; that letter sounds make words; and that preschool children learn the Alphabet through play and coloring.
	HOW TO TEACH CHILDREN TO READ This book introduces children to 86 phonetic sounds of the English language with a step-by-step plan to teach a child of any age how to read. How To Teach Children To Read also introduces the 220 Dolch word list (sight words) so that a child will be able to read, write and spell most written words.
	TEACH YOUR CHILD TO READ – VOWELS -PHONICS and SIGHT WORDS This book teaches 60 blended phonetic sounds; the 220 Dolch Sight or Whole Word list; and how to read three, four or more letter words.
	TEACH YOUR CHILD TO READ – ALPHABET PHONICS – SHORT ENTENCES This book is for parents and people with little or no teaching experience; and is presented in an easy-to- follow play-based method that any child can follow. Teach your child to read alphabet letter phonic sounds in short sentences, by sounding out short three and four-letter word sentences. After learning the alphabet sounds, vowels and Sight Words; this book puts that knowledge into practice.

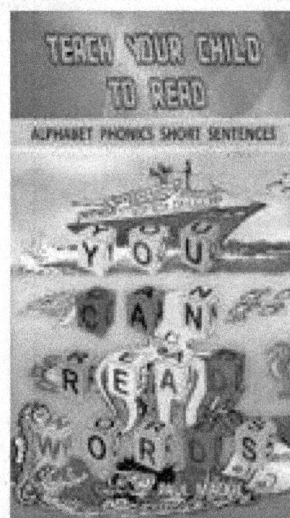

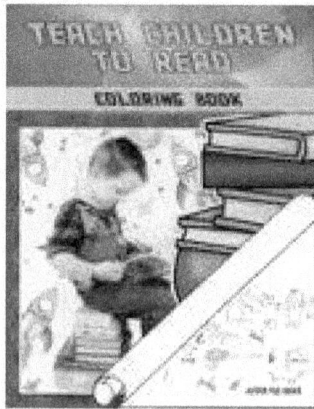

TEACH YOUR CHILD TO READ COLORING BOOK

This book is a coloring book with a combination of coloring book pages from How To Teach Children To Read, Alphabet Park.

This book has other activities that introduce children to the Alphabet letter sounds (phonics) and sight words needed to be able to read and write most English written words.

PRE SCHOOL COLORING AND PUZZLE BOOK

This coloring book is designed to help pre-school children with the following possible benefits: increase creativity; a free time activity; a transitional activity; a soothing distraction; improve fine motor skills; calm and center the mind; stimulate the brain and the senses; help focus the mind in the moment: and take the mind off distracting thoughts.

MOTIVATIONAL COLORING PUZZLE BOOK

This book has inspirational pictures, comic art, and puzzles for children, adults and seniors.
It is the author's hope that readers may experience some of the following benefits: give children a calming activity; help children learn to read and write; increase creativity; challenge thinking skills; reduce stress; improve state of wellness; improve fine motor skills; calm and center the mind.

ADULT AND CHILDREN COLORING BOOK

A 128 page adult and children coloring and puzzle book. The pictures and puzzles are printable for any age group, from adult coloring to children.

This book was designed for my 42-year-old daughter who had a stroke and has limited movement and communication due to her stroke. This book is helping her use both hands; improve her fine motor skills; and improve logical thinking skills.

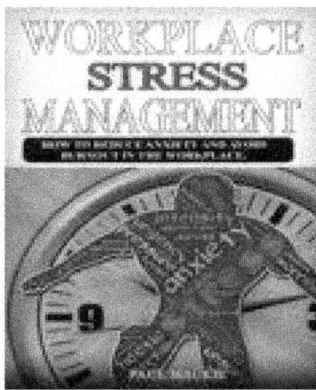

	WORKPLACE STRESS MANAGEMENT Do you feel stressed and anxious at work? You're about to discover easy to do workplace stress management activities to reduce stress, anxiety, and the possibility of a nervous breakdown in the workplace. You will Learn: a 5-minute exercise to start and finish your day; practical, easy to learn movements to help reduce workplace stress.
	GETTING THROUGH YOUR DAY Getting Through Your Day- Motivational Activities to help you reduce stress, be alert, in the moment, energized, and living a full life. This book introduces you to a 5-minute movement-based exercise to start your day. You will learn to focus the mind, energize the body and be ready for a meaningful day.
	BEST WAY TO TEACH YOUR CHILD TO READ This book introduces you to movement and play-based ways to help children develop the physical and other skills to learn how to read and write. The methods used in this book are Phonics; pre-primer sight words; developmental movements; the Balance Board; telling stories; and crossing the body's midline when reading or writing.
	FUN DAY FOR SENIORS Thousands of activities to help seniors be alert, in the moment, energized and living a full life.

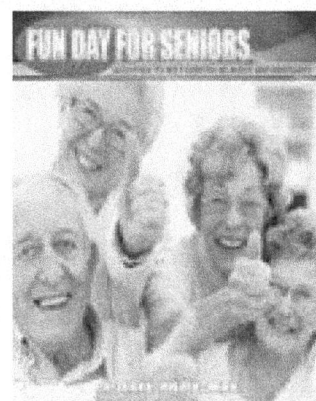

ABOUT THE AUTHOR

The author (Paul Mackie) has over twenty years of experience working with children and adults as an educator, and personal care worker.

Paul is a certified Early Childhood Educator in British Columbia, and a level two Early Childhood educator in Alberta Canada.

Paul has worked as a Community Care worker with special needs children, adults and seniors; and has worked with children in Daycares, Day Programs, and the School System.

The author has had several careers, with certification as a Marine Engineer; Industrial Millwright, Welder; Early Childhood Educator; with experience as a Teacher's Assistant; Special Needs Childcare Worker; Brain Gym Instructor; Senior Building Manager; with courses of study such as "The writing Road to Reading", "Accelerated Learning" and other Brain development courses.

The author is now retired from his last position as Senior Building Manager for a non-profit housing society.

For a free flipbook copy of "Play-Based Ways To Teach Your Child To Read";
and access to the "Early Childhood Development FORUM"
Visit: https://preschoolsurvivalguide.com/

Or
To see all the author's other books visit:
http://howtoteachchildrentoread.ca/

or
Please feel free to leave a review on Amazon
https://www.amazon.com/-/e/B0713QH79J

or
Contact me at: educationalchildsplay@gmail.com
the author's email to ask any questions about preschool child development.

Have a great day.
Paul Mackie

www.ingramcontent.com/pod-product-compliance
Lightning Source LLC
Chambersburg PA
CBHW081538040426
42447CB00014B/3424